GW00734459

Why is it cold today?

Written by
Alison Niblo and Hazel Songhurst

Illustrated by Robin Lawrie

Designed by Ross Thomson

Watts
LONDON • NEW YORK • SYDNEY

Is it cold today?
When it is very cold you can
see frost on the ground.

Sometimes snow falls from the sky.

2

The frost makes fern shapes

Try this

Pour warm water into a dish and cover it with a clear plate. Put the dish in the freezer. After a few hours, take out the plate. Little drops of water will have frozen on it and made frost.

Ponds and lakes turn to ice.

Snow forms high up in the air.
It is made of tiny ice crystals.
The ice crystals join together
to make snowflakes that fall
to the ground.

*ice
crystals*

When snow covers the ground it acts like a blanket. It stops heat escaping and keeps the soil from freezing.

Try this

See how much space snow takes up. Find two jars exactly the same size. Fill one up with water. Fill the other with snow, or use frost from the freezer. Wait for the snow to melt. What do you notice?

When you feel cold you shiver.
Sometimes your teeth chatter.
You can see your warm breath
like smoke in the cold air.

In cold weather, people wear thick clothes to keep warm. Animals grow thick fur to keep out the cold.

Try this

Find some clothes you wear when it is cold. Find some clothes for when it is hot. Choose a piece of clothing from each pile. Wrap one around each hand. Which hand is warmer? Which clothes keep you warmest?

T-shirt

wool scarf

It is cold in winter. This is one of the four seasons. The seasons after winter are spring, summer and autumn.

Try this

Put out food and water for the birds that stay behind in winter. You can buy wild bird seed or put out pieces of bread, apple or bacon. How many different kinds of birds visit your garden each day?

burrow

In winter some animals hide away from the cold in warm burrows. Many birds fly away to warm countries.

The seasons happen as the Earth moves in a circle around the Sun. The Sun's strongest rays shine on different parts of the Earth as it goes round. It takes one year for the Earth to circle the Sun once.

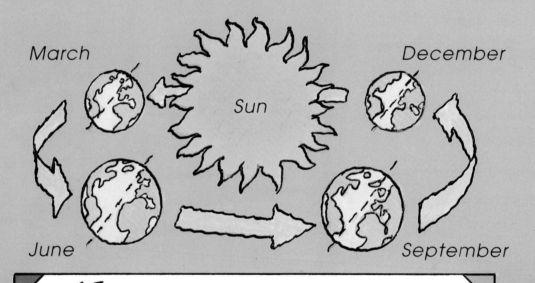

March

Sun

December

June

September

Try this

Close your eyes and turn your face to the Sun. Does it feel warm? Is the top of your head cooler than your face? It is like summer on your face and winter on your head.

The Axis is an imaginary line through the centre of the Earth. The Axis is tilted, so the Earth leans over as it travels around the Sun.

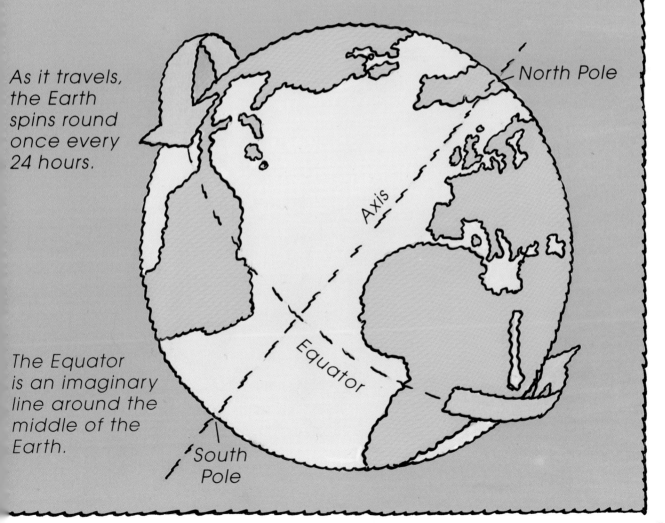

As it travels, the Earth spins round once every 24 hours.

North Pole

Axis

Equator

The Equator is an imaginary line around the middle of the Earth.

South Pole

When the North Pole tilts towards the Sun it is summer in the top half of the Earth, or Northern Hemisphere.

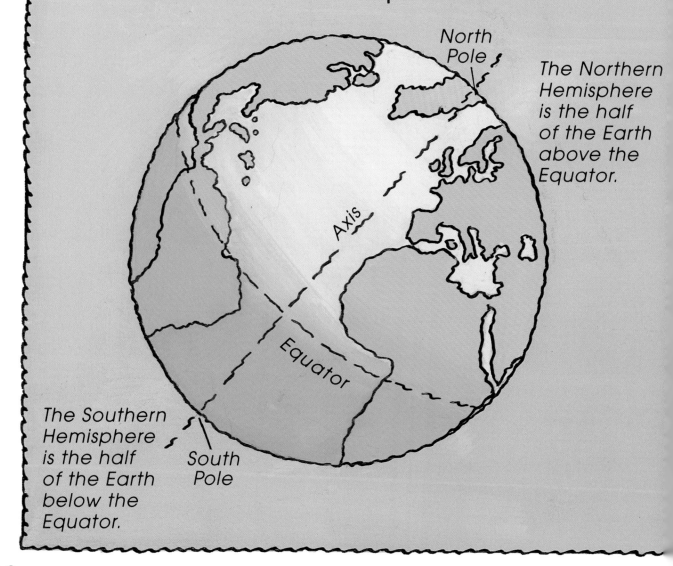

North Pole

The Northern Hemisphere is the half of the Earth above the Equator.

Axis

Equator

The Southern Hemisphere is the half of the Earth below the Equator.

South Pole

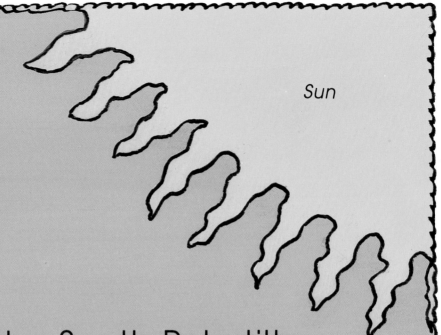

Sun

When the South Pole tilts towards the Sun it is summer in the bottom half of the Earth, or Southern Hemisphere.

Try this

Divide a large circle into four sections, spring, summer, autumn and winter. In each section draw a picture of what you like to do best in each season.

winter spring autumn summer

Australia and Europe are on
opposite halves of the Earth.
It is summer in Australia
when it is winter in Europe.
In Australia, people can spend
Christmas Day at the beach.

Try this

Look for Australia and Europe on a globe. Now look for your own country. Is it in the Northern Hemisphere - the top half of the Earth, or in the Southern Hemisphere - the bottom half of the Earth?

The season that comes after winter is spring. It happens in the parts of the Earth that are slowly turning towards the Sun's strongest rays.

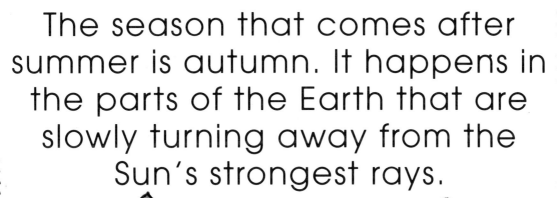

The season that comes after summer is autumn. It happens in the parts of the Earth that are slowly turning away from the Sun's strongest rays.

Try this

Collect some fallen leaves. Lay them between two pieces of paper. Put the paper in a pile of heavy books. Wait for a week, then glue the pressed leaves on to pieces of card.

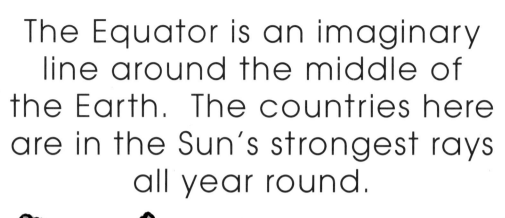

The Equator is an imaginary
line around the middle of
the Earth. The countries here
are in the Sun's strongest rays
all year round.

Try this

Fruit often has labels to show where it comes from. Next time you go shopping make a list of fruit from hot countries and fruit from cold countries. Can you think why fruit from hot countries would not grow well in Britain?

The Sun's strongest rays never land on the North and South Poles. These parts of the Earth are always cold. They are so cold that some of the sea freezes and makes giant pieces of ice called icebergs.

Try this

Make a small iceberg. Fill a balloon with water and leave it in the freezer for 24 hours. Take it out and peel away the balloon to leave a large piece of ice. Put it in a bowl of water. Does it float? How much of it is under the water?

The South Pole, or Antarctic, is the coldest place on Earth. Even in the middle of summer the temperature is below freezing.

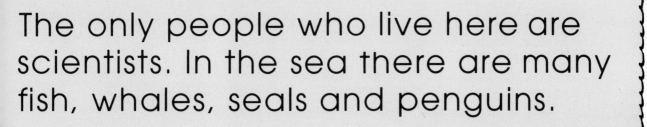

The only people who live here are scientists. In the sea there are many fish, whales, seals and penguins.

Try this

Find 3 empty yoghurt pots. Put an ice cube in each. Leave one pot in the fridge, one near a radiator or in sunlight, and one in the middle of the room. Which ice cube takes longest to melt? Can you think why?

INDEX

Animals 7, 9, 23
Antarctic 22
Australia 14
Autumn 8, 17
Axis 11

Birds 9

Christmas Day 14

Earth 10, 11, 14, 16, 17, 18, 20, 22
Equator 11, 18
Europe 14

Frost 2

Ice 3, 20
Ice crystals 4
Icebergs 2

North Pole 11, 12, 20, 21
Northern Hemisphere 12

Seasons 8, 10
Snow 2, 4, 5
Snowflakes 4, 5

South Pole 11, 13, 20, 21
Spring 8, 16
Southern Hemisphere 13
Summer 8, 12, 13, 14, 17
Sun 10, 11, 16, 17, 18, 20
Sun's rays 10, 16, 17, 18, 20

Produced by Zigzag Publishing Ltd,
The Barn, Randolph's Farm, Brighton Road,
Hurstpierpoint, West Sussex BN6 9EL, England

Consultant: Dr Anne Qualter, Centre for
Research in Primary Science and Technology,
Liverpool University

Editors: Janet De Saulles and Hazel Songhurst
Senior Editor: Nicola Wright
Series Concept: Tony Potter

Colour separations: Scan Trans, Singapore
Printer: G. Canale & Co. SpA., Italy

First published in 1993 in the UK by Watts Books
This edition 1995.

Copyright © 1993 Zigzag Publishing Ltd

BRITISH LIBRARY CATALOGUING IN PUBLICATION DATA A CIP
catalogue record for this book is available from the
British Library

Dewey Decimal Classification 551.57

ISBN 0 7496 1178 2